WEST CHICAGO PUBLIC LIBRARY DISTRICT
3 6653 00177 9325

# Astronomers:

From Copernicus to Crisp

by Connie Jankowski

**Science Contributor**

Sally Ride Science

**Science Consultants**

Nancy McKeown, Planetary Geologist

William B. Rice, Engineering Geologist

Developed with contributions from Sally Ride Science™

Sally Ride Science™ is an innovative content company dedicated to fueling young people's interests in science.

Our publications and programs provide opportunities for students and teachers to explore the captivating world of science—from astrobiology to zoology.

We bring science to life and show young people that science is creative, collaborative, fascinating, and fun.

To learn more, visit www.SallyRideScience.com

First hardcover edition published in 2009 by
Compass Point Books
151 Good Counsel Drive
P.O. Box 669
Mankato, MN 56002-0669

Editor: Mari Bolte
Designer: Heidi Thompson
Editorial Contributor: Sue Vander Hook

Art Director: LuAnn Ascheman-Adams
Creative Director: Keith Griffin
Editorial Director: Nick Healy
Managing Editor: Catherine Neitge


Printed in the United States of America.

This book was manufactured with paper containing at least 10 percent post-consumer waste.

Library of Congress Cataloging-in-Publication Data
Jankowski, Connie.
Astronomers : from Copernicus to Crisp / by Connie Jankowski.
p. cm. — (Mission: Science)
Includes index.
ISBN 978-0-7565-3965-8 (library binding)
1. Astronomers—Biography—Juvenile literature. I. Title. II. Series.
QB35.J36 2009
520.92'2—dc22 2008008325

Visit Compass Point Books on the Internet at *www.compasspointbooks.com*
or e-mail your request to *custserv@compasspointbooks.com*

# Table of Contents

# The Growing Universe

Did you know that the universe is getting bigger? Thanks to astronomers, our view of the universe is getting bigger, too. Their work has helped us learn about what exists beyond Earth.

Much of what we know about other planets comes from images taken by cameras on powerful telescopes. Telescopes allow us to see things far away—things we could never see without help. They allow us to look at other planets in our solar system. They have changed our view of the universe.

People in this book have also changed our views. Their studies have helped us see beyond our own planet and make us wonder, "What else might be out there?"

Edwin Hubble is just one of the many astronomers who changed the way we look at the sky.

## Did You Know?

Scientists like Edwin Hubble developed the theory of the Big Bang. This theory states that our universe came into existence between 12 billion and 14 billion years ago. At one point it was very small, hot, and dense, and somehow expanded to become the universe we know today. The universe will continue to expand and change.

# The First Astronomers

Until recently, people did not know much about outer space. The planets and stars were great mysteries to people on Earth. Shepherds, sailors, and travelers were the first astronomers. They made many discoveries. However, some of their ideas were not correct.

Most people thought Earth was flat. They believed that Earth was the center of the universe. Some even thought that the planets had magical powers.

Copernicus' model of the universe placed the sun at the center of the solar system.

# Nicolaus Copernicus (1473-1543)

The science of studying heavenly bodies—stars, the sun, moons, and planets—is called astronomy. One of the first astronomers was Nicolaus Copernicus. He was a Polish scientist who argued that the planets in our solar system move around the sun.

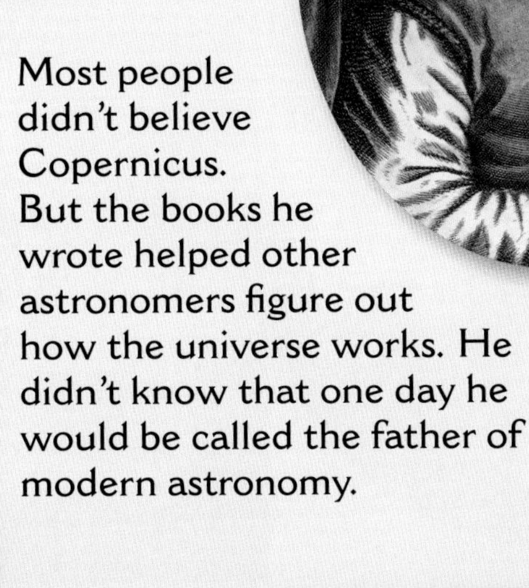

Most people didn't believe Copernicus. But the books he wrote helped other astronomers figure out how the universe works. He didn't know that one day he would be called the father of modern astronomy.

In 1491, Copernicus enrolled at the University of Kraków in Poland, where he first learned about astronomy.

# Galileo Galilei (1564–1642)

Galileo's first telescope could magnify objects three times larger than normal.

An Italian scientist named Galileo Galilei is credited with building one of the first telescopes. The first telescope was built by a Danish scientist in 1608. Galileo heard about it and soon built a much improved one. With his invention, he discovered mountains and craters on the moon, and watched stars and planets. He proved that Copernicus had been right—the planets did revolve around the sun.

People respect Galileo today. During his life, people did not want to hear his ideas. The Catholic Church insisted that Earth was the center of the universe. The church put Galileo on trial in 1633. He was held under house arrest for the rest of his life.

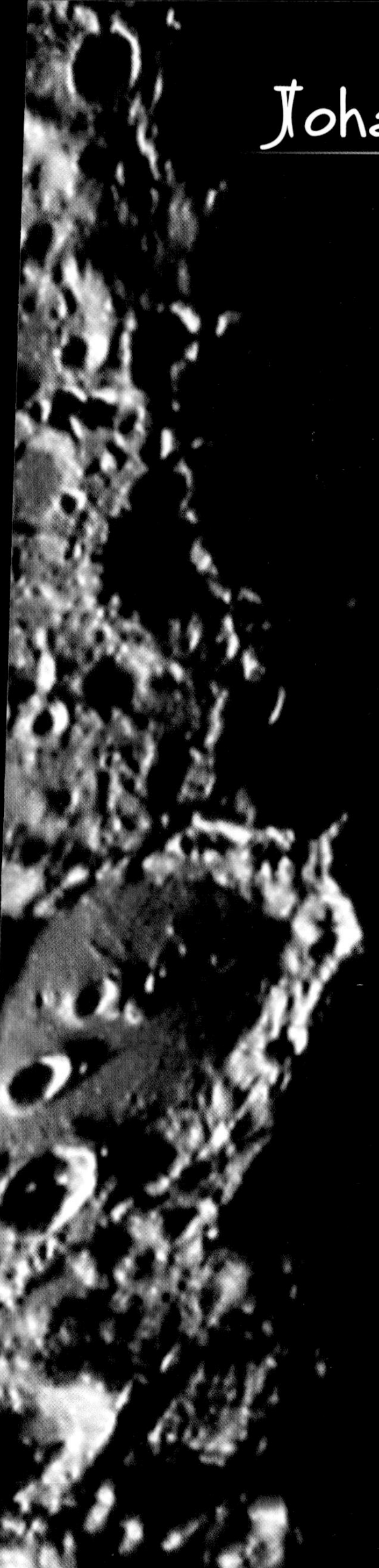

# Johannes Kepler (1571-1630)

Johannes Kepler was a German astronomer and mathematician. He believed that Earth was not the center of the universe. Kepler studied how fast and in what shape planets orbit the sun. These ideas are known as Kepler's Laws. Kepler was so important to the history of astronomy that craters on both the moon and Mars are named after him.

Although there were many people who studied space, the greatest advances in astronomy—such as the discoveries of Uranus, Neptune, and Pluto—would not occur for many years. These discoveries came from important astronomers who used telescopes to make impressive finds.

# Benjamin Banneker (1731-1806)

Benjamin Banneker is considered to be the first African-American astronomer. Growing up, he had always wondered about the stars.

In 1783, a friend offered Banneker astronomy lessons and loaned him books and instruments to study outer space. Banneker used these tools to teach himself about the sky.

In 1789, he began writing an almanac that contained information about the position of the sun, moon, and planets for every day of a year.

Because of his race, no one would publish his almanacs. Even without a willing printer, he continued to create one each year. In his almanacs, Banneker included essays, advice, and weather predictions. He also included his opinion about race and slavery in the United States. His first almanac was finally published in late 1791, and the books sold out until his last published almanac in 1797.

# Mary Fairfax Somerville (1780-1872)

Mary Fairfax Somerville was born in Scotland at a time that discouraged women from learning about science. When she became a rich widow at a young age, she was free to pursue her own interests. She loved science and decided to study astronomy.

Somerville's studies led her to conduct her own research. In 1826, she became the first woman to present her own scientific research to the Royal Astronomical Society in England. In 1835, she and Caroline Herschel became the first female members. The author of several science books, Somerville published her last at the age of 89.

# Maria Mitchell (1818–1889)

American astronomer Maria Mitchell is famous for discovering the first "telescopic comet," a comet too faint to be seen from Earth without the assistance of a telescope. She began watching stars at a young age in her father's observatory. Mitchell helped him with his work. In 1847, Mitchell discovered what would later be known as Miss Mitchell's Comet. Not only was she the first person in America to see a comet, but she also became the first woman to be named to the Academy of Arts and Sciences in 1848. In 1865, she was hired as the first faculty member in the astronomy department at Vassar College. This also made her the first female astronomy professor.

Maria Mitchell was the second woman ever to discover a comet. Caroline Herschel was the first.

# Annie Jump Cannon (1863-1941)

Annie Jump Cannon suffered a childhood case of scarlet fever that left her nearly deaf. However, that didn't stop the American-born scientist from doing what she wanted to do. In college, she studied physics and astronomy. She eventually went to work for Edward Pickering, a physicist and astronomer, at the Harvard College Observatory.

Pickering's goal was to record all the stars that had been seen in the sky. Cannon was one of the female astronomers who were hired to help. These women, who would become known as "Pickering's Girls," were called "computers" because they used math to locate stars. Together, the astronomers recorded more than 400,000 stars. Cannon found a way to group stars that is still used today. Between 1911 and 1915, Cannon classified 5,000 stars per month.

# George Ellery Hale (1868–1938)

George Ellery Hale became one of the most important astronomers of the 20th century—and with only a four-year college degree. Most top scientists go to school for a very long time. Not Hale. Much of what he learned, he figured out on his own. He even invented a tool to study the surface of the sun. He would eventually be known as the founding father of modern astronomy.

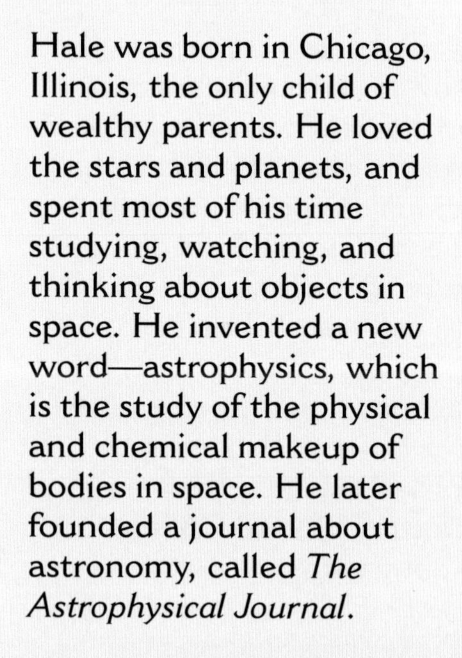

Hale was born in Chicago, Illinois, the only child of wealthy parents. He loved the stars and planets, and spent most of his time studying, watching, and thinking about objects in space. He invented a new word—astrophysics, which is the study of the physical and chemical makeup of bodies in space. He later founded a journal about astronomy, called *The Astrophysical Journal*.

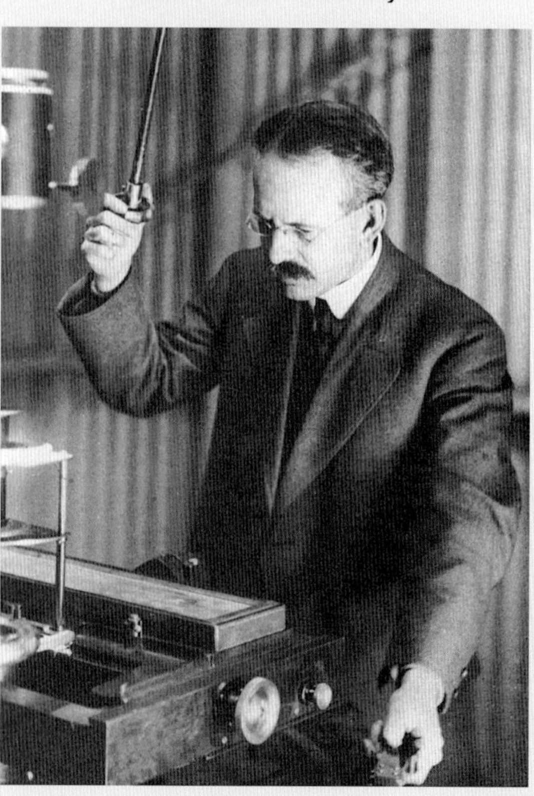

Hale founded three great observatories. In 1895, Hale helped design the Yerkes Observatory in Wisconsin. In 1904, he founded the Mount Wilson Observatory near Los Angeles. He then helped build the first giant reflecting telescope. The telescope used mirrors instead of lenses and measured 200 inches (5 meters) long. It was installed at the Mount Palomar Observatory in California. Named the Hale Telescope, it was the biggest telescope in the world for more than 40 years.

Hale's observatories led the field of astronomy for many years. Discovery after discovery was made in Hale's observatories. Scientists used Hale's research to learn about galaxies and what they are made of. They learned new things about the sun.

Hale's greatest achievement is not so much what he knew. It's what he did. By building his observatories, he ensured that future astronomers would have somewhere to work and continue their studies in the field of astronomy.

At the time of its construction, Yerkes Observatory was the most modern observatory in the world.

# Edwin Hubble (1889–1953)

An American scientist named Edwin Hubble was one of the greatest astronomers of all time. He changed our view of the universe. As a boy, he imagined other worlds through books such as Jules Verne's *20,000 Leagues Under the Sea* and Henry Rider Haggard's *King Solomon's Mines*. These stories opened his mind to science.

Edwin Hubble worked at the Mount Wilson Observatory after World War I.

Hubble almost took a different career path by going to law school. He practiced law for a few years, but law did not make him happy. He knew he wanted to study outer space, so he went back to school to train in astronomy.

His work in science was sidetracked once more when he became a soldier in World War I. When the war was over, he was finally able to follow his heart. He took a job in an observatory. There Hubble found that there are other galaxies in the universe. He created a system to group these galaxies. He developed Hubble's Law in 1929. This law proved that the universe is still growing.

Hubble worked from a 100-inch (2.5-m) telescope, the best available at the time. Today's astronomers use much more powerful telescopes. They also use telescopes in orbit above Earth. One of the most important instruments in the history of astronomy is named in his honor—the Hubble Space Telescope.

## NASA's Four Great Observatories

NASA has four Great Observatories: the Hubble Space Telescope (1990), the Compton Gamma Ray Observatory (1991), the Chandra X-Ray Observatory (1999), and the Spitzer Space Telescope (2003). These observatories are stationed in space, and each houses a large, powerful telescope. Each telescope has a different specialization. In 2000, the Compton was brought out of orbit because of a broken part.

The Spitzer Space Telescope can see "stellar nurseries," where young stars are born.

# Subrahmanyan Chandrasekhar (1910–1995)

In 1983, astronomer Subrahmanyan Chandrasekhar was awarded the Nobel Prize in physics. The Indian-born scientist discovered that when stars lose their energy, they collapse and become dense. They become white dwarf stars, neutron stars, or black holes. A white dwarf is a small, dense, hot star near the end of its life. A neutron star is a small, dense star made up of tightly packed neutrons. A black hole is an area in space where gravity is so strong that even light cannot escape from it.

In 1999, NASA named the Chandra X-Ray Observatory in his honor. The satellite observatory is one of NASA's four Great Observatories.

Nothing can escape from a black hole—not even light.

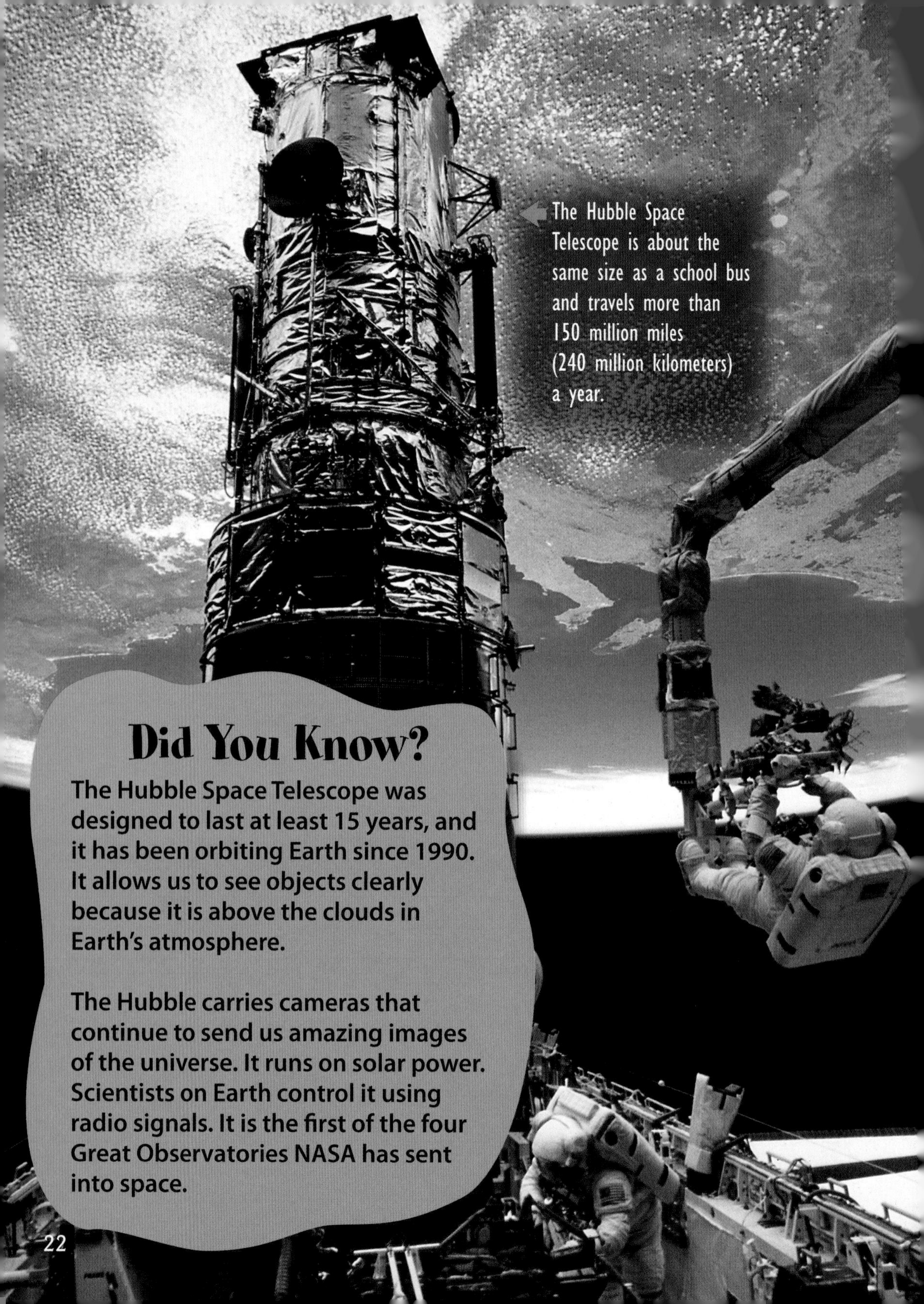

The Hubble Space Telescope is about the same size as a school bus and travels more than 150 million miles (240 million kilometers) a year.

## Did You Know?

The Hubble Space Telescope was designed to last at least 15 years, and it has been orbiting Earth since 1990. It allows us to see objects clearly because it is above the clouds in Earth's atmosphere.

The Hubble carries cameras that continue to send us amazing images of the universe. It runs on solar power. Scientists on Earth control it using radio signals. It is the first of the four Great Observatories NASA has sent into space.

# Lyman Spitzer Jr. (1914–1997)

Lyman Spitzer Jr. was one of the 20th century's great scientists. He was the first to propose placing telescopes in space. Born in Ohio in 1914, Spitzer studied physics and taught at Princeton University for almost 50 years. He was known as a great teacher. Spitzer was one of the world's leading experts on interstellar matter—the gas and dust between stars. He studied how stars and galaxies formed from this material. He also founded a lab that works on using nuclear fusion, the source of a star's energy, to produce energy on Earth.

In 1946, Spitzer suggested that an observatory in space would show much clearer images than telescopes on the ground. This was more than a decade before NASA began developing Spitzer's ideas and the first satellite was launched. In 1990, 44 years after he first proposed it, Spitzer saw his dream become a reality. The Hubble Space Telescope was sent into space.

## In Honor of Spitzer

**NASA named the last of its four Great Observatories after Spitzer, the man who first came up with the idea of putting telescopes in space. The Spitzer Space Telescope was launched in 2003. It uses infrared light to help astronomers see through clouds of dust in space. It has discovered new galaxies. It may also have recorded a faint image of the youngest star ever observed.**

# Margaret Burbidge (1919- )

British physicist Margaret Burbidge is an important astronomer for many reasons. Her work added to our understanding of the rotations and masses of galaxies. She helped figure out how elements are formed inside stars.

She fought for career opportunities for other female astronomers. Burbidge is especially important to the Hubble Space Telescope—she helped design some of its original instruments.

A female astronomer at work in the early 1900s

At 380 miles (608 km) above Earth's surface, the Hubble Space Telescope takes thousands of images of our planet and sends them to astronomers.

## Did You Know?

The Hubble Space Telescope orbits Earth at a rate of 5 miles (8 km) per second. It gets its power supply from the sun and uses the same amount of energy as 28 100-watt light bulbs.

## What a Telescope Sees

There are five types of telescopes in outer space: radio, infrared, optical, X-ray, and gamma ray. Each telescope takes images unique to its type. Large telescopes will show more objects with sharper images than small telescopes.

## Carl Sagan (1934–1996)

Few people have made as big an impact on astronomy as Carl Sagan. The American-born scientist made astronomy popular with the general public. He wrote books about space. His book *Cosmos* was the best-selling science book ever published in English. He also produced a television show that accompanied the book.

Sagan won a Pulitzer Prize, an Emmy, and a Peabody award for his work, and one of his novels, *Contact*, was made into a movie. He worked on many of NASA's unmanned space missions. When he died, the landing site of the Mars Pathfinder spacecraft was renamed the Carl Sagan Memorial Station in his honor.

## Beatrice Tinsley (1941–1981)

Born in England and raised in New Zealand, Beatrice Tinsley led a short but important life. She studied galaxies and the age of stars. She won many awards for her work before dying of cancer. After her death, a group of astronomers began a new award in her honor: the Beatrice M. Tinsley Prize, which is awarded for outstanding creative contributions to astronomy or astrophysics.

# Jocelyn Bell Burnell (1943- )

The thought that we might one day receive signals from alien life has always been fascinating. In 1967, Jocelyn Bell Burnell thought she might have found just that.

Bell Burnell was a university student in her native England. She worked with her adviser to help build a large telescope. Their goal for the telescope was to pick up radio signals from space.

The radio telescope that Bell Burnell helped build was so big that 57 tennis courts could fit on land covered by it. She collected data in the form of lines on strips of paper. Bell Burnell studied more than 400 feet (122 m) of chart paper from the telescope every four days.

From this data, Bell Burnell found signals that could not be explained. She and her teacher had no idea what the pulsing signals were. They named them Little Green Men, or LGM. They thought they could be from aliens.

Soon after, they discovered that a spinning neutron star can make the pulsing signals. These stars became known as pulsars.

Bell Burnell is now the head of the physics department at Open University in England. She has received many awards for her work. Her teacher received the Nobel Prize in physics in 1974 for the discovery of pulsars.

# Mars Project Scientist: Joy Crisp

**NASA Jet Propulsion Laboratory**

## Rock and Rover

How do NASA geologists study rocks millions of miles away on Mars? Joy Crisp did it with help from two busy little rovers.

As a girl, Joy Crisp loved English, reading, and math. In college, she took a lot of math classes. But she couldn't see herself as a math teacher. A geology class sparked her interest and helped her choose her profession.

Scientists can't travel to Mars, so they sent robotic rovers to be their eyes and ears. Crisp led a team that decided what tools to give the rovers. The tools were used to analyze Mars' geology—its rocks and soil. The rovers made exciting discoveries. Some parts of Mars were once covered in water.

"We knew we wanted to look for things on rocks like ripple marks from water," Crisp says. Crisp's team chose cameras, drills, and other tools for the rovers. These tools identified minerals formed in water.

## On the Job

If you were a geologist, you would study rocks and learn about the land and how it formed. As a geologist, you could also:

- investigate fossils hidden in rocks. Fossils help scientists understand the creatures that once lived on Earth and on other planets.
- figure out where water, minerals, or diamonds are located.
- come up with solutions to environmental problems, including soil and beach erosion.

## How Do They Know?

Crisp and her team studied photographs of Mars' rocks. The rocks look similar to ones on Earth that have been changed by water. Find a rock that's been shaped by water. How would you describe it?

The rovers roamed Mars' rocky hills and rolled into its craters. They scraped rocks and snapped photographs. They beamed the data back to scientists on Earth. It proved that Mars, the red planet, was also once a wet planet.

The robots Crisp's team sent searched for evidence that water once existed on Mars.

# Astronomers at a Glance

## Benjamin Banneker

**Fields of study:** *Astronomy, mathematics, clockmaking, publishing*

**Known for:** *Being the first African-American astronomer*

**Nationality:** *American*

**Birthplace:** *Maryland Colony*

**Date of birth:** *November 9, 1731*

**Date of death:** *October 9, 1806*

**Awards and honors:** *The Benjamin Banneker Historical Park and Museum, built in 1998 in Baltimore, Maryland*

## Jocelyn Bell Burnell

**Field of study:** *Astronomy*

**Known for:** *Discovering pulsars*

**Nationality:** *British*

**Birthplace:** *Belfast, Northern Ireland*

**Date of birth:** *July 15, 1943 (born Susan Jocelyn Bell)*

**Awards and honors:** *Beatrice M. Tinsley Prize, American Astronomical Society, 1987; Herschel Medal, Royal Astronomical Society, 1987; Commander of the British Empire (for services to astronomy), 1999*

## Margaret Burbidge

**Fields of study:** *Astronomy, mathematics*

**Known for:** *Designing part of the Hubble Telescope; president of the American Association for the Advancement of Science and the American Astronomical Society; director of the Royal Greenwich Observatory*

**Nationality:** *British*

**Birthplace:** *England*

**Date of birth:** *August 12, 1919*

**Awards and honors:** *Fellow, Royal Society of London, 1964; Annie J. Cannon Award, 1972 (refused it because it was only given to women); Bruce Medal, Astronomical Society Pacific, 1982; National Medal of Science, 1984; Albert Einstein World Award of Science Medal, 1988*

## Annie Jump Cannon

**Field of study:** *Astronomy, physics*

**Known as:** *Census Taker of the Sky*

**Known for:** *Developing the star classification; first woman to receive doctorate in astronomy (Groningen University, 1921); first female officer of the American Astronomical Society*

**Nationality:** *American*

**Birthplace:** *Dover, Delaware*

**Date of birth:** *December 11, 1863*

**Date of death:** *April 13, 1941*

**Awards and honors:** *First female honorary doctorate from Oxford University, 1925; Henry Draper Medal, National Academy of Sciences, 1931; Cannon crater on the moon and Annie J. Cannon award given by the American Association of University Women named for her*

## Subrahmanyan Chandrasekhar

**Field of study:** *Astrophysics*

**Known for:** *Working on the structure and evolution of stars*

**Nationality:** *Born British Indian; became naturalized American citizen in 1953*

**Birthplace:** *Punjab Lahore, British India (now in Pakistan)*

**Date of birth:** *October 19, 1910*

**Date of death:** *August 21, 1995*

**Awards and honors:** *National Medal of Science, awarded by President Lyndon B. Johnson, 1967; Nobel Prize in physics, 1983; Copley Medal, Royal Society of London, 1984*

## Nicolaus Copernicus

**Field of study:** *Astronomy*

**Known as:** *Father of modern astronomy*

**Nationality:** *Polish*

**Birthplace:** *Torún, Poland*

**Date of birth:** *February 18, 1473*

**Date of death:** *May 24, 1543*

**Awards and honors:** *Nicolaus Copernicus University in Torún, Poland, Copernicus Award, given by the Armed Forces Communications and Electronics Association/U.S. Naval Institute, third orbiting astronomical observatory, and crater on the moon all named for him*

## Joy Crisp

**Fields of study:** *Geology, robotics*

**Known for:** *Creating tools used to analyze Mars' geology*

**Nationality:** *American*

**Birthplace:** *Colorado Springs, Colorado*

**Date of birth:** *1958*

**Awards and honors:** *NASA Group Achievement Awards, 1997 and 2005; Exceptional Service Medal, 2004*

## Galileo Galilei

**Field of study:** *Astronomy, physics, mathematics, philosophy*

**Known as:** *Father of modern science*

**Known for:** *Building a superior telescope; challenging accepted beliefs about outer space*

**Nationality:** *Italian*

**Birthplace:** *Pisa, Italy*

**Date of birth:** *February 15, 1564*

**Date of death:** *January 8, 1642*

**Awards and honors:** *Galileo Galilei Award, given by the International Commission for Optics, lunar crater, and* Galileo Orbiter *spacecraft named for him*

## George Ellery Hale

**Field of study:** *Astronomy*

**Known for:** *Naming astrophysics; founder of three observatories*

**Nationality:** *American*

**Birthplace:** *Chicago, Illinois*

**Date of birth:** *June 29, 1868*

**Date of death:** *February 21, 1938*

**Awards and honors:** *Henry Draper Medal, 1904; Gold Medal of the Royal Astronomical Society, 1904; Bruce Medal, 1916; Galileo Award, 1920; Copley Medal, 1932; Hale Telescope, asteroid, craters on the moon and Mars, and solar cycle all named for him*

## Edwin Hubble

**Field of study:** *Astronomy*

**Known for:** *Discovering other galaxies*

**Nationality:** *American*

**Birthplace:** *Marshfield, Missouri*

**Date of birth:** *November 29, 1889*

**Date of death:** *September 28, 1953*

**Awards and honors:** *Bruce Medal, 1938; Gold Medal of the Royal Astronomical Society, 1940; asteroid, crater on the moon, and Hubble Space Telescope all named for him*

## Johannes Kepler

**Fields of study:** *Astronomy, mathematics*

**Known for:** *Three Laws of Planetary Motion*

**Nationality:** *German*

**Birthplace:** *Stuttgart, Germany*

**Date of birth:** *December 27, 1571*

**Date of death:** *November 15, 1630*

**Awards and honors:** *Johannes Kepler Award, given by the Institute of Navigation, and the Johannes Kepler University in Austria both named for him*

## Maria Mitchell

**Field of study:** *Astronomy*

**Known for:** *Discovering a telescopic comet*

**Nationality:** *American*

**Date of birth:** *August 1, 1818*

**Birthplace:** *Nantucket, Massachusetts*

**Date of death:** *June 28, 1889*

**Awards and honors:** *Gold Medal from the king of Denmark, 1848; inducted into the New York Hall of Fame, National Women's Hall of Fame, and the Hall of Fame for Great Americans; Comet Mitchell and the Maria Mitchell Association named for her*

## Carl Sagan

**Field of study:** *Astronomy*

**Known for:** *Popularizing astronomy and other natural sciences*

**Nationality:** *American*

**Date of birth:** *November 9, 1934*

**Birthplace:** *Brooklyn, New York*

**Date of death:** *December 20, 1996*

**Awards and honors:** *Pulitzer Prize, 1978; Peabody Award, 1980; Emmy awards, 1981; NASA Exceptional Scientific Achievement Medal, asteroid, Carl Sagan Center for the Study of Life in the Cosmos, Carl Sagan Memorial Award, and the Carl Sagan Award for Public Understanding of Science named for him; Mars Pathfinder renamed Carl Sagan Memorial Station in honor of him*

## Mary Fairfax Somerville

**Field of study:** *Astronomy*

**Known for:** *First woman to present original scientific research to the Royal Astronomical Society*

**Known as:** *The Queen of Science*

**Nationality:** *Scottish*

**Birthplace:** *Jenburgh, Scotland*

**Date of birth:** *December 26, 1780*

**Date of death:** *November 28, 1872*

**Awards and honors:** *First college for women at Oxford University named for her*

## Lyman Spitzer Jr.

**Field of study:** *Astronomy*

**Known for:** *First proposing to send telescopes into outer space*

**Nationality:** *American*

**Date of birth:** *June 26, 1914*

**Birthplace:** *Toledo, Ohio*

**Date of death:** *March 31, 1997*

**Awards and honors:** *Bruce Medal, 1973; Henry Draper Medal, 1974; Gold Medal of the Royal Astronomical Society, 1978; National Medal of Science, 1979; asteroid and Spitzer Space telescope named for him*

## Beatrice Tinsley

**Field of study:** *Astronomy*

**Known for:** *Studying how galaxies change over time*

**Nationality:** *New Zealander*

**Date of birth:** *January 27, 1941*

**Birthplace:** *England*

**Date of death:** *March 23, 1981*

**Awards and honors:** *Beatrice M. Tinsley award named for her*

# Glossary

**astronomer**—person who studies celestial objects

**astronomy**—study of the universe and objects in space such as the moon, sun, planets, and stars

**astrophysics**—study of the physics and chemistry of bodies in space

**atmosphere**—blanket of gases that surrounds a planet

**black hole**—invisible region in space with a strong gravitational field

**Chandra X-ray Observatory**—NASA satellite that observes things in space, such as black holes and neutron stars

**comet**—icy and dusty object that orbits a star

**Compton Gamma Ray**—NASA satellite that collected data on high-energy physical processes occuring in the universe

**gravity**—force of attraction between two objects

**Hubble Space Telescope**—NASA satellite that observes things in space with ultraviolet, visual, and near-infrared wavelengths

**infrared light**—invisible light waves just longer than red light waves on the electromagnetic spectrum

**interstellar matter**—dust and other matter, including streams of protons, moving between the stars

**Kepler's Law**—series of three laws that explain planetary motion

**NASA**—U.S. National Aeronautics and Space Administration

**neutron star**—small, superdense star that is composed mostly of tightly packed neutrons

**nuclear fusion**—atomic nuclei combining to form a larger nucleus, usually releasing energy

**observatory**—buildings designed to study outer space

**orbit**—path of one body around another

**physics**—science of matter and energy and interactions between the two

**planet**—celestial body that orbits a star and is the only object in its orbit

**pulsar**—spinning neutron stars that give off bursts of radio waves at regular intervals

**radiation**—emission of energy waves

**solar system**—planets and other bodies orbiting the sun; other planets around other stars are called planetary systems

**Spitzer Space Telescope**—NASA satellite that uses infrared radiation to observe small stars and molecules in space

**star**—huge ball of gas that produces heat and light

**telescope**—instrument made of lenses and mirrors that is used to view distant objects with cathode rays

**white dwarf**—small star that has run out of fuel

# Astronomy Through Time

| | |
|---|---|
| **2296 B.C.** | Chinese record earliest comet sighting |
| **1530 A.D.** | Nicolaus Copernicus writes *On the Revolutions of the Heavenly Spheres* |
| **1577** | Tycho Brahe views a comet, inspiring him to draw a cosmic model of the sky with Earth as the center of the universe |
| **1605** | Johannes Kepler formulates his Three Laws of Planetary Motion |
| **1608** | Dutchman Hans Lippershey applies for a patent for the first telescope |
| **1610** | Galileo Galilei uses a telescope to observe heavenly bodies and discovers four largest satellites of Jupiter |
| **1786** | Caroline Herschel is the first woman to discover a comet |
| **1839** | The Harvard College Observatory, the first official observatory in the United States, is built |
| **1895** | George Ellery Hale founds *The Astrophysical Journal* |
| **1925** | Annie Jump Cannon receives the first and only honorary doctorate given to a woman by Oxford University in England |
| **1929** | Edwin Hubble formulates Hubble's Law, which helps astronomers determine the age and growth of the universe |

| | |
|---|---|
| **1948** | The Hale Telescope is opened on Mount Palomar, California |
| **1957** | Soviet Union launches *Sputnik 1*, the world's first artificial satellite, into space, beginning the Space Age |
| **1958** | Eager to join the Space Age, the United States forms the National Aeronautics and Space Administration (NASA) |
| **1969** | Americans Neil Armstrong and Buzz Aldrin are the first humans to land on the moon |
| **1972** | Margaret Burbidge declines the Annie J. Cannon award because it is only awarded to women |
| **1983** | Sally Ride becomes the first American woman and the youngest American astronaut to enter outer space |
| **1990** | The Hubble Space Telescope is launched into space, 44 years after Lyman Spitzer Jr. first proposed the idea |
| **2006** | Astronomers decide there are only eight planets in our solar system and reclassify Pluto as a dwarf planet |
| **2008** | A powerful gamma ray burst becomes the most distant object ever seen with the naked eye; the explosion occured 7.5 billion years ago |

# Additional Resources

Briggs, Carole S. *Women Space Pioneers*. Minneapolis: Lerner Publications Co., 2005.

Somervill, Barbara A. *Nicolaus Copernicus: Father of Modern Astronomy*. Minneapolis: Compass Point Books, 2005.

Spangenburg, Ray, and Kit Moser. *Carl Sagan: A Biography*. Westport, Conn.: Greenwood Publishing Group, 2004.

Voelkel, James R. *Johannes Kepler and the New Astronomy*. New York: Oxford University Press, 1999.

Weatherly, Myra. *Benjamin Banneker: American Scientific Pioneer*. Minneapolis: Compass Point Books, 2006.

Zannos, Susan. *Edwin Hubble and the Theory of the Expanding Universe*. Hockessin, Del.: Mitchell Lane Publishers, 2004.

## On the Web

For more information on this topic, use FactHound.

1. Go to *www.facthound.com*

2. Type in this book ID: 075653965X

3. Click on the *Fetch It* button.

FactHound will find the best Web sites for you.

# Index

# About the Author

## Connie Jankowski

Connie Jankowski is a seasoned journalist, marketing expert, public relations consultant, and teacher. Her education includes a Bachelor of Arts from the University of Pittsburgh and graduate study at Pitt. She has worked in publishing, public relations, and marketing for the last 25 years. She is the author of 11 books and hundreds of magazine articles.

## Image Credits

SuperStock, Inc., cover (left), 10 (left), 32 (middle, Galileo); Bettman/Corbis, cover (right), 15, 31 (top); Getty Images, 2; NASA, 3, 20, 22, 23 (bottom), 25, 27, 29 (front), 30 (bottom), 32 (top); Jurgen Ziewe/Shutterstock, 6–7; The Print Collector/Alamy, 6 (front), 8-9, 16, 33 (middle, Hale); The Granger Collection, New York, 9 (top), 10 (right), 11 (front), 31 (bottom), 33 (top); Vieloryb/Shutterstock, 9 (bottom); Thomas Ward/Shutterstock, 11 (back); Courtesy of the Banneker-Douglass Museum, Annapolis, Maryland, 12, 30 (top); Library of Congress, 13 (front), 34 (top); William Attard cCarthy/Shutterstock, 13 (back); F. Carter Smith/Sygma/Corbis, 14 (back); NOAA, 14 (front), 33 (middle); Robert Goode/Shutterstock, 17; New York Times Co./Getty Images, 18 (front), 32 (bottom); Roger Ressmeyer/Corbis, 18-19; William Franklin Mcmahon/Time & Life Pictures/Getty Images, 21 (top), 31 (middle); Christ Butler/Photo Researchers, Inc., 21 (bottom); Time & Life Pictures/Geyy Images, 23 (top), 34 (middle); Hulton Archive/Getty Images, 24 (top), 30 (middle); Wellesley College Archives, 24 (bottom); Tony Korody/Sygma/Corbis, 26 (top), 33 (bottom); Courtesy of David and Theodora Lee-Smith, 26 (bottom), 34 (bottom); NASA/Photo Researchers, Inc., 29 (back).

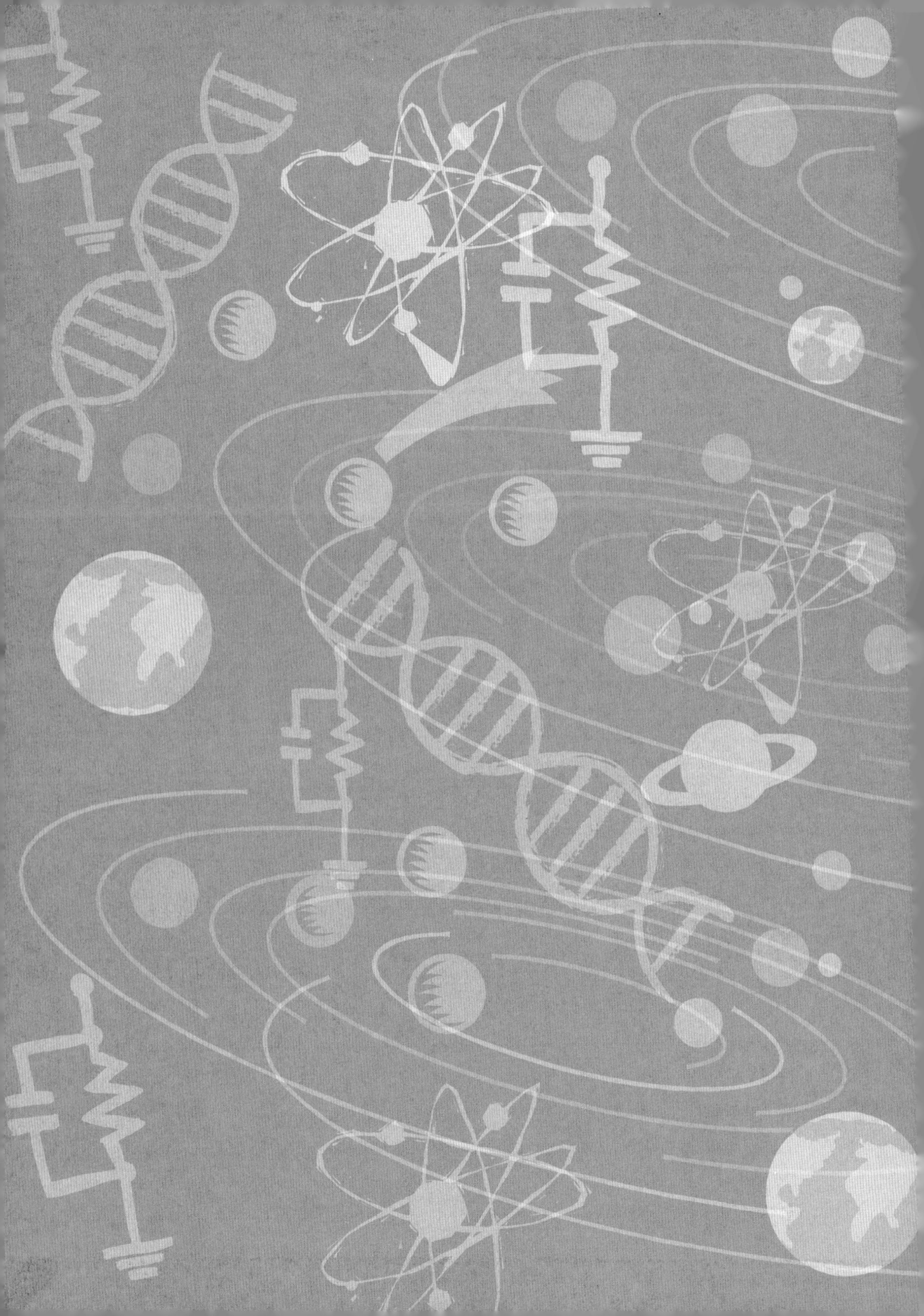